Zacchaeus

Luke 18:35–19:9 for Children

Written by Loyal A. Kolbrek
Illustrated by James Needham

ARCH® Books
Copyright © 1994 Concordia Publishing House
3558 S. Jefferson Avenue, St. Louis, MO 63118-3968
Manufactured in the United States of America

When Jesus came to Jericho,
Folks followed in a crowd.
Some of them were silent,
But some became quite loud.

They pleaded with the Savior
To heal them where they hurt.
Some so weak they couldn't stand
Were lying in the dirt.

Broken bodies, twisted limbs,
Eyes that could not see;
Now and then a feeble cry,
"Have mercy, Lord, on me."

The Savior loved them, every one,
And knew their faith was true.
He healed them with a gentle touch;
Their bodies, then, like new.

One man who gathered taxes
Was called a Publican.
The way he lived, he seemed to be
A very wealthy man.

The people all looked down on him,
For he was very short.
Zacchaeus had no friends in town;
They didn't like his sort.

Suddenly a shout went up:
"Jesus is coming near!"
And people ran to line the road,
Pushing to see and hear.

Zacchaeus saw the crowd and said,
"I wish that I were tall.
I'm much too small for this big crowd;
I cannot see at all."

Zacchaeus ran ahead and saw
A large and spacious tree.
He said, "I'll find a sturdy branch.
Then I can really see."

Zacchaeus climbed this sycamore
And watched the dusty trail.
He waited for the Lord to pass;
He'd see Him without fail.

The Lord looked up into the tree,
And people heard Him say,
"Zacchaeus, you come down here.
I'll visit you today!"

The crowd began to grumble,
"Should Jesus eat with him?
Zacchaeus lies and cheats us.
His life is full of sin.

"He steals a certain portion
Of taxes that we pay.
His purse is overflowing;
He gets richer every day!"

They didn't think the Savior
Should visit in his home.
They thought it would be better
To leave this crook alone.

Zacchaeus was quite flustered
At what the people said,
And as he walked with Jesus,
He simply bowed his head.

At home he turned to Jesus
And said, "I'm going to share
Half of my possessions
With those who need my care.

"And if I've cheated anyone,
I'll pay him four times more.
People here will see I've changed
From what I was before."

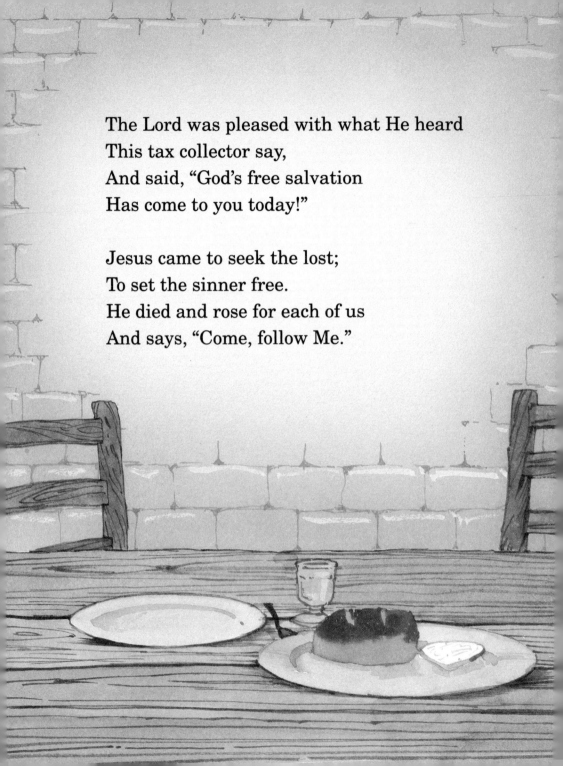

The Lord was pleased with what He heard
This tax collector say,
And said, "God's free salvation
Has come to you today!"

Jesus came to seek the lost;
To set the sinner free.
He died and rose for each of us
And says, "Come, follow Me."

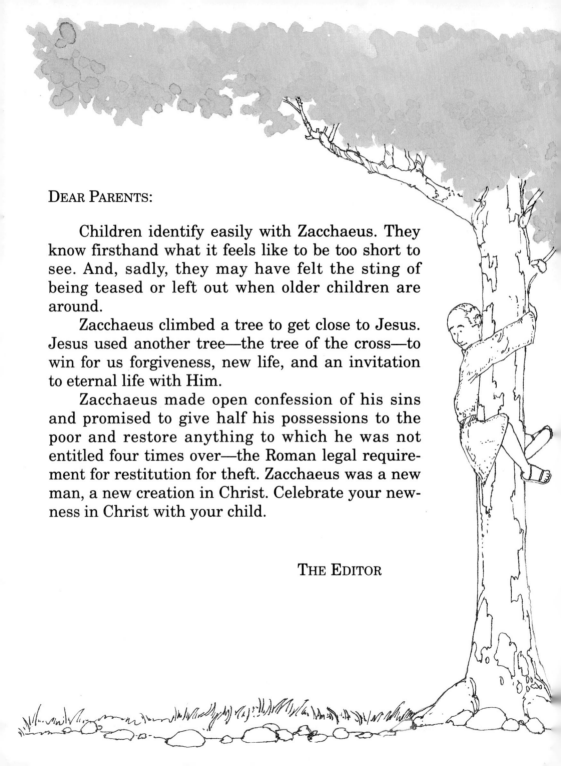

DEAR PARENTS:

Children identify easily with Zacchaeus. They know firsthand what it feels like to be too short to see. And, sadly, they may have felt the sting of being teased or left out when older children are around.

Zacchaeus climbed a tree to get close to Jesus. Jesus used another tree—the tree of the cross—to win for us forgiveness, new life, and an invitation to eternal life with Him.

Zacchaeus made open confession of his sins and promised to give half his possessions to the poor and restore anything to which he was not entitled four times over—the Roman legal requirement for restitution for theft. Zacchaeus was a new man, a new creation in Christ. Celebrate your newness in Christ with your child.

THE EDITOR